EBURY PRE

GIRL TO GODDESS

Nishi is a poetess, spoken-word artist and content creator on a mission to help people find their inner voice. She believes that we're all hidden goddesses and angels who have forgotten our self-worth. To help people discover their true self, Nishi started voicing her realizations on Instagram under the pen name goddesswrites. Her debut book, *Girl to Goddess*, takes people on her own journey of mistakes, failures, fears, lessons, perspectives and realizations of life, love and everything in between. You can visit her on Instagram, @goddesswrites.

Celebrating 35 Years of
Penguin Random House India

A JOURNEY OF SELF-DISCOVERY, SELF-LOVE & SELF-WORTH

GIRL TO GODDESS

NISHI

EBURY
PRESS

An imprint of Penguin Random House

EBURY PRESS

USA | Canada | UK | Ireland | Australia
New Zealand | India | South Africa | China

Ebury Press is part of the Penguin Random House group of companies
whose addresses can be found at global.penguinrandomhouse.com

Published by Penguin Random House India Pvt. Ltd
4th Floor, Capital Tower 1, MG Road,
Gurugram 122 002, Haryana, India

First published in Ebury Press by Penguin Random House India 2023

10 9 8 7 6 5 4 3 2 1

ISBN 9780143460619

Typeset in Sabon by Manipal Technologies Limited, Manipal
Printed at Thomson Press India Ltd, New Delhi

www.penguin.co.in

To the divinity that resides in us

Post pictures of your favourite pages from this book on social media or share your own journey and experiences using #girltogoddessbook so I can see them and feature them on my Instagram page @goddesswrites.

Contents

CONTENTS

Someone asked me, why do you feel the need to write? Who is even going to read your book? Honestly, I don't know who will read this or who won't. But I feel that only words allow me to breathe now. This voice that is suppressed inside my heart chokes me.

I have lived a quarter of my life as a human, and it has only made me realize that our perception that 'being born as a human is a blessing' is wrong. I believe the earth is not all good. Maybe we're all trapped on this planet and are being punished for our past-life karma by living a human life. Humans are so complicated. The more we age, the more this life gets on our nerves. A lot of people don't even feel like living and breathing in this world any more. Every day becomes a task to find some source of happiness and motivation to get through this day. Every night becomes a task to fight the demons inside our heads and the nightmares we can't seem to forget.

But amidst all of this, I also realized that the good thing about being a human, and probably the only thing that sets us apart, is our sixth sense. Call it intuition, conscience or inner voice. Since the day I discovered that voice within me, I knew that, from this day, my life wouldn't be the same. I found the divinity that resides in me and I realized it is guiding me every second. And so, I decided to name that voice 'GODDESS'. Now, I can support myself and say, 'Come what may, I've got this.' The journey of healing begins here. I hope that, with me, you too will join this journey and find the goddess/angel within you.

GIRL

Girl Arrives

Where am I?
What am I?
Who am I?
I don't remember a lot.
I have questions
and this is where I shall begin.
This is where I arrive
to find the answers
to find my home.

—*Arrival*

I heard
it'll be a beautiful place to be
but I am not sure still.
It's all dark in here
sometimes silent
often noisy
but I'm getting the hang of it.
Maybe it'll be beautiful outside
maybe it'll be worth the wait
maybe I'll find the light
and maybe it won't be so lonely.

—Hope

Since I was in the womb
I have been hearing the noises
the screams, the abuses, and
the voices of violence.
Labouring out of the womb,
I realized
I have been so used to those noises
that they started to soothe me.
Listening to my mom's rants
about her hard-to-survive life
literally calmed me.
My tears would stop
listening to her sorrows.
Since then,
while noise would comfort
peace discomforted me.
Maybe this deafening world
is where I belonged
but to my mother,
I was the silver lining.
So here I am
taking the chaotic birth
only to be the calm to my mother hereafter.

—*Beginning*

They call me a girl
I don't know what that means
some seem happy
some not very
I don't understand
if they want me or not
but I'd like to believe
I am sent here
with a purpose.

—*I hope I am not wrong*

I am learning and laughing
crying and trying
growing and understanding
but this is not as easy
as it seemed.
This world and its people
are complex and complicated
manipulative and manipulated
and I don't seem to get
any of it.
It's just been a dozen years
but it feels like forever,
is it okay to wish
that I can go back
from wherever I came?

—I am scared

I wanted to believe my mother
every time she said,
my girl is the most beautiful thing
on this earth.
But only I knew from the inside
how painful was
the price of this beauty.

—Unprotected

One house
Fourteen humans
each of them called me
different names,
gave me different labels,
skinny, brown, petite, ugly, short
and words I could hardly utter.
I was a human
and so were they
then why did they disgust me?
they weren't the reason why I exist
then why did they laugh upon
my existence?

—The family we called

Girl Bleeds

GIRL TO GODDESS

I have always kept my face down
in respect to the ones regarded high.
Little did I know
they'd reciprocate my gesture
by looking down upon me.

Do not tell anyone
do not share
do not speak of it.
What has happened has happened,
keep the honour of the home.

—Hush . . .

Ssshhhhh . . .
be quiet
don't let your cry make a noise
mute your screams
drink up your tears
don't utter a word
press your pain under your chest
hide somewhere in the dark.
If you fail to
then,
you'll too
end up like your mom
with a sore body.

I didn't silence myself,
my voice muted
in their embrace.

—*Loyally stabbed*

I was too young and naive
to understand,
there's a price to pay
for everything you wish for.
I remember there were days
my soul craved some heart-to-heart
I yearned for good conversations
to be specific,
I wanted to be wooed by flattering words.
But I was too young to understand
that this was an expensive demand.
Little did I know
this exchange
would make me rip off my clothes,
surrender my naked body
and act submissive to their lustful wants.
Let me be clear,
It's not that they made me do it
It was a deal that I agreed to,
without negotiating.
Because all I needed was
a collection of verbal validation
a fulfilling conversation.

—*Permanent stain*

I was an absolute disappointment for so many
What am I good for?
the question I was asked frequently
they tried to make sense of my existence
but I failed them
'Who will even love me?'
they wondered.
and now I'm also dying in the thirst
to be looked at with love and tenderness
to prove them wrong
to assure myself—I'm NOT a failure.

Girl Loves

I was his beginning
and he was my endgame.

—*The forever story I imagined*

NISHI

Maybe not all is dark in this world
maybe love is truly the light we all need.
Hold me close,
make me exclusively yours.

Why do I stare at you without blinking?

So that I don't miss out on the minuscule bits of
your beauty. My eyes just want to take it all in. My
eyes try to find answers for why I feel awestruck
looking at you. I want to see and show you a part of
you which is yet to be discovered by the world and
yourself. I hope now you won't mind my gaze.

—*Obsession*

You love me because of us,
so why not
from now on
instead of saying I love you,
you rather tell me I love us.
I would like to hear that on repeat,

I Love Us.

Pour yourself into my wounds
and I shall be healed.

—You're my magic potion

Is it okay to be afraid of losing someone you love?

Umm, I think maybe it's good to fear that. You don't take your love for granted. You keep loving them until you overpower your fear.

The fear of losing itself is a realization of how much you want them in your life and how you can't imagine a day without them.

So, I guess it's okay to fear, but it's not okay to stop loving.

—*Decoding fears*

It's beautiful that love is endless but it's upsetting that we must make efforts to win in love every day. With love, even these efforts have become endless too. In our effortful days sometimes these efforts exhaust me, drain me, and make me indifferent to all the feelings. Some days I don't want to give or receive love at all. Some days I am okay with love taking a back seat.

Some days I'm just tired of losing myself in loving you. Some days I don't feel like loving you and I don't know if it is okay to feel so.

—*Burn out*

If heartbreak and its ache
is to be suffered in silence
then, love and its euphoria
should be screamed out loud, right?
I think
I could never understand
what it was with you.

She remembers the flaws they showed her.
She accepts hatred towards her,
but what she forgot is
how to accept the bouquets of admiration for her.
Maybe you could bring 365 ways to appreciate her
for 365 days. Voice your praises for her. Applaud
loudly. Compliment that extra in her.
She remembers her flaws. Help her forget.
Beautify her with your words. Love her back.

There's nothing right in us
yet, our love doesn't feel even a bit wrong to me.

—*Delusional me*

Why am I caught up so intensely?
albeit having ample reason
to give you up
I land up squeezed in your arms
losing myself bit by bit in you
whenever we meet.
I don't know why
but I keep longing
to return to the place
I call my home,

your heart.

Have you ever felt,
you're there with them but you're not?
They feel you are there for them
sitting right next to them,
but your mind isn't really into them.
You're busy thinking:
'I have love, I have this relationship,
I have a routine, I have us, then what's still missing,
why am I not satisfied yet . . .'
Interrupting you from your thoughts,
they suddenly call your name, and you realize,
that's your name! That's you.

YOU'RE MISSING.
You are lost in finding you.
What a tragedy!

Girl Hurts

My brain is so conflicted with double thoughts right now. My heart is sending signals to my head to not fall apart from you, but my body is saying you're not going to change, and the pain is not worth the love we have. 'Cause this pain is only one-sided. It's destroying only me.

Keep me alive, please. Stay with me for me. I surrender all of me to you for my survival. I let you choose the way to save me. I let you.

—Surrender to survive

It's so frustrating
when I need you in your absence.
When I tell you
and you can't do anything about it.
You don't know when I say I need you
it means I NEED YOU.

I could've loved you from afar without mingling into
any sort of relationship. But I chose to be bound in
love with you because I felt the need for you in my
life. I felt it was okay to depend on you emotionally
without any regrets. You complete me. Why don't
you understand it's just so difficult when you're not
around? And that I NEED YOU and Only YOU?

How ironic is it that one person in this billion-people world was fighting with you to save you, to love you, to be with you at any cost and you called it suffocation. While I was fighting for us, you were all set to give up on me.

I wonder why you couldn't understand. That it was my determination in love that you called suffocation for you.

—Not my fault if I love too much

You're holding too tight
even if it's with love
I'm hurt and it's hurting
wish I could escape.

I had mistaken your cage
for embrace.
and you clasped,
wish I could escape.

My heart longs for you
but no love oozes out.
my body is weary
wish I could escape.

You consumed my heart and head and body,
now I don't find a way
to go back to square one
Wish I could escape.
To return, reset and resume.

—*Caged in love*

I never was out of your sight.
maybe this validates the reason
you forgot to miss me.

—*Taken for granted*

I'm not celebrated
I'm not enough
I'm merely an instrument
to meet your whims.

You don't love my soul,
it's just your body
bridging the gap
by responding to mine.

Now it's echoing in my head
This is not love!
But . . .

this heart is still not giving up
It still doesn't stop from
believing in you and in love.

Someone said,
we are all made from the same stardust
our core fabric of being is the same.
Then what made you indifferent to me?
Are you not a human?

You're the best and the worst
that happened to me.
Are you, *my karma*?

44

It's not the mistakes you made that broke me. It's the lies after lies after lies to hide those mistakes that broke me to an extent where I'm beyond repair now. I'm not the culprit who causes pain. A devil neither.

I'm a human who has been murdered with lies again and again. I'm shattered into pieces from fighting for us. I survived every day to devote my life to you. I have all the courage to embrace the evilest of you, the darkest of you. Just don't use your lies to choke me. I'm a feared soul. Dreaded by you.

Please, no more lies.

If the eyes are a window to the soul,
how did I see love
in the eyes of a monster?
wait,
was it just the reflection of my own eyes?
was it all my love?

I know I'm not enough for you
my insecurities have started showing up
but my love is not possessive. Yes, my trust issues are
real, but they are not beyond our love.

I know my love is conditional, for my only condition
is to love me more. But I know that can't be fulfilled
unconditionally.

Yes, I know I'm falling deeper into your love each
day,
but I am no one to bind you, I'll have to let you go
and let this end.

—*Conversations with myself at 3 a.m.*

Is it okay if I don't want to share a piece of me with
anyone?
Not even you.
If I want a piece of me to be hidden.
It could be some of my words or thoughts
or a piece of clothing or one of my hobbies.
Now, the question here is,
why should I hide it from you,
when you are my everything?

Because, I want my soul to feel special about itself
knowing that at least all of me is not out there,
something between me and my soul is still safe with
the other. Who knows, one day that secret could
become the reason for me to stay alive when you are
not there.

Let me keep this secret sacred with my soul, please.
Is it okay?

She was the victim
yet committed the crime
of embracing the criminal
who attempted to murder her heart,
time and again.

—Strangled in love

Tears are rolling down your face
you're crying
although you don't want to,
they don't seem to stop.
I know it's difficult to even breathe with this feeling
that you are left alone.
But I want you to know that
your body is giving you proof with these tears
that you loved them unconditionally.
Your love for them was pure.
You didn't fail them in love,
they failed you.
You might have made some mistakes
but it wasn't entirely your fault.
you exhausted your soul
in trying again and again
to save it from falling apart
to not lose hope in 'happily ever after'
but the truth is,
maybe you deserved better.
and you should realize this about yourself
it'll bring you some peace.
The burning in your soul will lessen a bit.

Girl Tries

Wish I could resume my life
wish I could start afresh.
But then I think
if I had resumed my life
it wouldn't have you
and I don't want to find another person like you
because I want YOU.
I know I'm conflicted
with my own thoughts
I'm into a troublesome phase
and it's quite a mess that I'm into.
But I realized, without you
it would only get messier
I think I forgot that
you are the calm to my chaos.
I can't let me delete you from my life
because I don't want someone like you.
I want YOU.

I can let go of the other things attached to me
but I can't let go of you.
You own a part of me
I'm paralysed without your existence
and your exit
would be the death of me.
I can't let go of you.
'Please don't go.'

—*Emergency*

When I was myself
you had a problem,
When you were yourself
I had a problem,
Now you have become I
And I—you
Yet nothing is sorted
So why not
you and I both build 'us'
and see if that works?

—*Making adjustments*

Listen,
Why don't you start my day by reminding me
how much I am loved
and I'll end it by reminding you
how much you're desired?
The regime of reassurance
Let's keep that going
and it will keep us going

Shall we?

I want you to choose me again and again.
I want you to choose me when I'm the hardest to
love,
I want you to choose me when I'm impossible to live
with.
I know, I made the worst of your worse.
I've been the devil to your angel.
But there were also times,
when I've been the nicer to your nice
and I've been the better to your good.
In the good, the bad, the beautiful, and the ugly,
I remained as your constant.
I made you my everything.
My passion for you never changed.
and so,
I want you to choose me again and again

I am worthy of you.

I am worthy of your love.

I think now I know how to resolve us. Whenever we have a fallout, we think distancing from each other would help. But I think distancing is just a sign of giving up. It's when breathing the same air in the same room resolves things for us. We are actually 'the closer the better' kind of people. Do not leave the room before resolving. Because outside the room we'll just drift apart. Resolve us, right here. There's nothing a hug can't fix. I hope you understand what I mean.

I'm not happy
I'm unable to feel you
You touched me
but I'm not fulfilled
I want to stand by
yet don't want to hold on.
I'm still flowing with you
for the efforts you take
for the promise I made
to not give up on you
until you're exhausted.
I'm sure, this is just a phase
I'll wait for it to pass
So that we can start
another
magical hour,
more beautiful than ever.

Someone asked me, what happens when you burn too much for love and extinguish?

I feel you but I think love is like a candle. The air might take away the light but that doesn't mean I can't light up the candle again.

Simple. Go light up your love. There is no peace in darkness.

I'll turn this body into an exotic destination
a sight you haven't seen before.
I promise
I will be the place you yearn to visit.
Will that make you extend your stay?

I'm okay about you leaving me in the night. The pillows hug me and absorb my tears. They help me pass the night. But the problem is I'm left alone in the daylight when I can't even confide in the pillow. I want to hide this heartache and show everyone that I'm okay. I don't want to tell people that they were right about you. Please appear again and live the lie with me. Please.

I've been at my worst with you,
You brought out all the madness in me
and the consequences of it.
Strangled, tired, feared, angered.
The reasons were enough to quit on you
but I couldn't
because even the wrong things
didn't feel wrong to me.
I would like to believe
that your fight was for love
So, even if I'm tired of loving you
I won't walk away
For I'm assuming
You always kept love above everything else
you kept us above everything else.

—Justifying you

Girl Burns

You very well knew,
my heart only pumps
love with ease.
Yet you clogged it
causing me pain
being reckless and ruthless about it.
Knowing your attempt to murder my heart
doesn't fall under any section of crime.

Every ounce of my cells
burns in loving you,
I die every night
and give birth to myself every morning again.
I create a core made of love
but again, you crush it to the core.
They say, love is easy, it simply happens.
If that is so,
then why is loving you so difficult for me?
Why do I die every night?
and give a painful birth to me every morning
To love you again?

—Burning in love

GIRL TO GODDESS

Now you're no more a star
your stroke doesn't light me.
You exploded eventually
turning yourself into a black hole.
Taking away my gleam,
sank me into your darkness
what a conscious trap!

I should have understood—how could you hear
the voices and muffled cries in my heart when you
couldn't even hear the echoes and screams of my
pain? I'm sorry for holding you more than you
wanted to be held. I should have understood you're
not worth keeping.

I will let you go. 'Cause you didn't care to see any efforts of mine taken for you to stay.

An irresponsible person like me, caring only about herself, held you responsibly with her love. I took the responsibility for your smile, your laughter, your tears of joy and your tears of pain. But now I can't make myself responsible again for making you stay longer than you need to. I will let you go.

You and I were
hanging by a thread.
I would lie in exhaustion
but wouldn't sleep,
holding my end of the thread.
No love,
no promises,
just hoping your hand would reach
to hold the other end.
But you loosened it
for me to tighten more
and that wounded me
to an extent
that I, myself, had to
let go of it.

The girl traded her body for love. For her naive self didn't understand the sacredness of the bodies becoming one. Even if the love was a lie, she wanted to feel it anyway. In living this lie, she sold her heart but was left with the scarred bones.

Girl Dies

You ripped off my body
tore the strip of my soul
but I couldn't say a word.
Because I thought
I needed to feel this pain
to prove my love to you.

But then I wonder
if my body fails to endure this pain
would you stay or
would you end up
in another's arms
singing a song of praise
in my memory?

—Are you worth dying for?

I synced my body with yours
but your mind couldn't with mine.
You were not ready to give
what I wanted
you simply offered
no commitments
no hopes
no promises
no love
and yet I complied,
do you know why?
Because,
my need of you as a person
was more than your need of me as an object.

All my doubts
my anxiety
my restlessness
my anger
my frustration
my screaming in tears
could go away
with just your one phone call
Why would you not do that?
Don't you understand
you have the power to save me
and you're not using it?

—*How cruel of you*

Humiliation wore down
the leftover beauty from my body.
My skin textured
like a barren location.
My body slouched
like a dead rose.
I was a stone
in the diamond full of people.
Nobody talked to me
In fact,
I was looked at
like a disgusted, cursed soul.

—Love can wear down your body

Do you know what was the price of our love?

The price I paid for our love was
'the love that existed in me for me'.
I emptied all of it without thinking about the time
when you would leave, how would I love myself
then?

I loved without any backup.
And it cost me my own existence.

You named me these,
And I believed them so.
I think I should remember them
and you won't have to repeat them to me again and
again.
Let me write them:

I'm selfish
I'm egoistic
I spit poison
I'm not trustworthy
I'm always wrong
I'm dumb
I'm a coward
I'm shallow
I'm worth hating

—The conditioning

TO

Choosing Darkness

When love entered,
why didn't the light?
I thought,
with love
light would fade my darkness
but it didn't.
So, now I think

maybe it wasn't love
maybe it was a made-to-believe
perception of love.

—*What a fool I made of myself*

I don't know why my heart is feeling heavy at this moment. In fact, it was like this the entire day. Where am I going, I don't know. Do I want to run and go ahead or be stuck where I am . . . I don't know. Why so many favours for the sake of love? Why can't love just be pure love? No future, no past, no promises, no commitment. Whatever is in the now, why can't we let it just be? Why am I kneeling in front of these emotions? Crying now and then. Is it the old me coming back? Is being vulnerable to love making me too weak? What is my strength? Whom do I want to be? What have I made of myself or is it you who has made me this?

—*Getting sick*

Let the curtains be closed.
Let the pillow soak up my tears.
Let me scowl and scream at my hurt.
I'm tired of the aching smiles.
Let my pain be vulnerable to the night.
In the absence of light,

Let *me* just *be*.

You admire the sunlight and sunshiny days.
Your eyes see everything dancing in the sun's rays
but what you don't know is,
that they're dancing to tunes played by someone else.
What you see in the daylight is not all real.
We all change with the sun rise and set.
People are often vulnerable in the dark hour.
The mask is worn off in the blackness of the nights.
The dark space is the outlet for many.
And so, I too empty all of it in this hour
to bear the sunlight once again.

Oh damn! You alarm.
Don't start again.
I don't want to be reminded of another new day.
The day doesn't have any newness anyway
and I don't want to create one either.
I'm still waking up with a yesterday in my head.
I'm bored of feeling
what I have been feeling for days now.
The tears don't stop
and the muscles in my head feel swollen.
I can't see what lies in the present.
The torture of the past few days
has worn off my body.
I can't move.
I'll go back to sleep again.
At least the emotions will be separated
from this body.
And I'd appreciate God
if I don't get to wake up the next day.

—*Morning thoughts*

I was looking at my eyes in the mirror today,
they had a lot of pain.
These eyes have seen a lot of failing days.
I tried; I'm trying again
yet failing at it miserably.
Seems like there is no last attempt to try.
Till when?
For how long?
Why is this not the ending?
Why is it so draining?

I don't know
yet,
Whom to call mine?
Because,
everything looks like a dream
when I'm awake,
I'm surrounded by no one
but emptiness.

These wet eyes are better in the dark.
They no longer can endure
the bright smiles
that prick my vision
and the pitiless laughter
that wrenches my gut.

The hurt was from many
I'm not sure if love from one
would make up for all.
and so,
the trial starts.

—Rebound

Revisiting Burns

I'm scrolling down my Instagram
insomniac but with groggy eyes
not knowing why these fingers don't stop
why is the heart restless,
why is it hollow?
what am I looking for?
whom am I waiting for?
nothing helps me to rest
this void wearing me down
asking me to find something
or someone to be filled with
loneliness isn't giving any peace
togetherness isn't a reality,
dear universe,
either answer these questions for me
or give me dreamless sleep.

You're gone.
now what's next?
I need you. I need you to live.
Please come back.
You made me so dependent on you and now left me
wondering what else to do with this life. This is what
the withdrawal of a person does.
Once we find that high in someone, we tend to ask
for more. And when that someone leaves, we jump
immediately to the next high for we don't know how
else to live.
I wonder, can someone's withdrawal help us to get
addicted to ourselves?
At least, there won't be any withdrawal then.

The truth is
if I haven't forgiven you yet
doesn't mean I haven't moved on.
It means
I have moved on
but
without healing completely.

—It is okay not to be okay about forgiving

Those feelings are buried
somewhere in the heart
over the years
but not dead.
That's why I haven't forgotten them yet
they still trigger
at the very thought of love.

We have a reason for why we do something. And I too had a reason to love filth like you. Lately I realized, you weren't my love interest. In fact, you were my escape from the painful life I was in. The hurt you gave was still more tolerable than the pain I was already in. But now I can see clearly it wasn't love. It was an illusion which faded with time.

You were just an escape I needed. To breathe and keep breathing. I held your hand so you could pull me into your fantasy land. Didn't matter if it was worse, because I was anyway living the worst.

—The reason I was with you

It's not that I don't have anything to share or I'm okay. Sometimes there's too much going on in my head that my words fail to explain. Sometimes I tell the thoughts to shut up. Sometimes I don't let my hands write about certain things even though I badly want to. I keep it inside me and do not let it come out because I fear, I fear—what if it gets manifested? What if all of it comes true?

Wish I could have a little more patience
before bursting out with fury,
raining judgements and complaints all over you
converting all the good times into bad ones
forgetting all the extraordinary love you flaunted
that I felt ever since our beginning
making our every day better or worse
but never the same.
Wish I had a little more patience
if I could hold myself that one day
I would have got a chance to see you in white,
Waiting for me in the car
one more time.

—Justifying you again

The truth is my heart did want
to put an end to you
the day you hurt me.
I wish some cosmic force
could make you disappear
like you never existed.
If it wasn't the withdrawal of your touch
I would have escaped from the relapse.
However, trust me
my heart did want an end of us.

—*The regrets*

It is our song that's playing now. You left me but the song and the memories attached to it didn't leave me. I crave to relive those moments I once lived with you. The cherished ones. But I understand that a little while can't be an excuse to get back to you once again.

After a long time, I'm on my own. And it's needed. So, I know how I would like to be loved when I fall in love with someone next time. Don't give yourself in until someone walks to you with a forever. Someone who doesn't want to know the way to exit your life.

I wish like my physical wounds I could show you my emotional bruises too. Each time I got hurt, how deeply it scarred me. If only I could show you my emotional wounds bleeding, maybe then you would understand how urgently I needed love to heal and recover from the hurt you gave me.

—The need to get fixed

What do I do now?
You told me to love you
without holding back,
I loved you
but you left.
The old wounds still stir my soul
and I feel broken.
But you deny fixing me
now who will save me?
Love couldn't,
now who will?

Feeling Tired

Hold on.
Why would I let you come back again?
You won't believe it, but the breakdowns you gave
me, give me chills to date. I'm still finding ways to
gather myself and heal. I'm sorry I'm not ready to go
through everything once again. Not even half of it.
Now it's not just about you. I think the tolerance for
anything wrong has ended in me with the end of you
from my life.

I don't know. I'm too tired of speaking, too tired of writing, too tired of feeling, too tired of listening to people saying, I'm there for you. Honestly, I don't need anyone right now. Whatsoever the situation is, let me be alone and try to fight it alone. I have led my whole life under influence: be it good or bad. Now I want to try to lead by myself. Please let me.

Yes, some days I will seek advice from you, but some days I don't want to be advised by anyone. Why is it so tough to believe that sometimes I don't need you, but I just need me and only me?

I need the courage to stop every wrong that's happening to me. I need the courage to save myself from falling for what can totally destroy me. I need the courage to make an exit from something that's making me even more miserable. I need the courage to begin again. Where do I find it? I don't have it in me to try again today. I hope when I wake up tomorrow, I can find it in me.

There's no escape from people's hurt,
they'll always find a way to cause you torment
either by suffocating you with too much love
or leaving you begging for love.

—*Human traits*

I don't want you to be with me to heal me.
But I want you to be with me to hear me.
The voices in my head want a listener
before they consume me
and I know only you can hear them.
Let me speak please.
Don't shut me down.
Just shut the noises in my head harassing me.
I don't expect you to be the light to my darkness.
But I expect you to listen to those noises calling you
out. Be my peace. I will seek my solutions and build
myself once again. Just hear me out.

Don't blame yourself
for being trapped with them
who bribed their love to you.
Don't blame yourself
for drowning in fake love
which was portrayed as surreal.
Don't blame yourself
for being raised at a place
where you were expected to
expect love the least.
None of it was your fault.

—Forgive yourself

Love isn't corrupted, love isn't complicated, love isn't difficult, love is as easy as breathing. Love is the core. Don't blame love. You're messed up. You compromised your values. You never understood the reality of love because of your own insecurities. Each one of us is blessed with an infinite capacity for love. Don't blame love when you yourself have cursed it.

—4 a.m. thoughts

I think I will have to move on without you. Because moving on with you isn't happening any more. Whenever you walk towards me, I see guilt and regret making their way towards me. The regret of falling for you. The guilt of giving all of me, over and over again. With you I will always be stuck. I can't fracture my soul and vanish all the love I have in me. So yes, it's decided. I'll move on without you.

I know this happens to a lot of us. Our past flashes at us randomly any time at any hour and it gives shivers to the body. I think it's time we stop our past from intimidating us any more and whenever it flashes, scream out loud that you're no more that person. You've become so much better than what you were. You are what you are now and what you are now defines you.

Rebooting Life

It's not the end,
if it has not got better yet.
Hang in there.

What if pain is keeping you alive and not really love?

I believe love keeps you in a bubble while pain
bursts the bubble and shows you there's still more to
yourself. You are not the one who you thought you
were. Pain helps you discover yourself, who you truly
are. Pain values happiness. Pain takes the healing
seriously. Pain makes you resilient to get through this
life. Pain is keeping us alive; I believe.

It's strange I didn't cry when you walked out of my life. You quit on me as if I was a wrong habit that you picked up. Yet I didn't cry as much as I cried while I was in love with you. But I think it shouldn't be strange when a person who's not meant to be with you, leaves. It is fine if you feel a relief as though the toxins are being released from your body and soul. It's not strange, it is the tendency of your body to feel light once the dirt is washed away.

Let my tears roll down
while you kiss me all over my face.
Don't question why my eyes are wet
I won't be able to explain.
But the least I can say is
It's helping.
I'm healing.

There are happy endings, there are sad endings but to some stories we forget to give an end or we leave it to destiny. We leave the endings unclosed. You shut the door without informing them. You think now that the doors are closed, you are set free. But you know what, just when you are about to start a new phase, they knock at your door and show you a recap of your past. Don't escape it if you don't want to make a sequel of your past. Get closure. Take the ending before a new beginning.

—Lesson learnt

Have you seen a half-cut tree
that looks nearly dead?
It's strange to say
but I have a resemblance to it.
Just like that tree
I'm also cut, broken, scarred,
and bruised by people for their wants.
You know what,
exactly like that tree
I look half-alive, half-dead.
But then we are not done yet.
We're still breathing,
the roots are holding strong.
The love for self is just buried,
not taken away.

—I'm not finished yet

Stop crying,
stop feeling pity for yourself.
Stop looking for possibilities to end this life.
You can still get this right.
It is still in your hands.
You are one decision away.
Decide.
So what if today was pathetic,
you can promise yourself to not cry tomorrow.
Do whatever it takes to get a hold of yourself.
Leave that hand that pulls you into the past.
Walk alone.
You've got this. Go ahead.

Come back to your senses. The ones who left you shouldn't hold you any more. Not even in your memories. I understand it is easier said than done. The memories keep coming to you time and again and at times you're helpless when those thoughts don't leave you. But what I believe is old memories can be replaced by new ones. You let out a cry for the old ones but also look forward to creating new ones for yourself. For your ease. Will you? For yourself?

—*Mirror talks*

No! You can't leave this world just like that. Not before you leave behind your name on people's tongues to remember you loud and clear. Wake up, muster up some courage to say yes to the things you were denying yourself till now, and to say no to the things you were nodding to before. You have lost enough; you can't leave this world before you win it all back. Turn the tables. Let's play the game again. And let's win this time.

Here's the truth.
Unless you fix yourself from your past,
there's no guarantee that you won't be tricked or
cheated again. And if that happens again, you'll be
left beyond repair. Don't make a fool of yourself
another time. Figure out your past. Learn from the
people who misguided you. Don't hurry to fall into
another relationship until you're steady. Don't choose
the suffering yet again when it's not worth it.

I asked someone how some people can stay always happy. Don't they get affected by any other emotions?

I was told that it's not that they are always happy. Yes, the façade seems happy and fulfilled but trust me it's all hollow inside. They have just arranged themselves, forming layer after layer, just like building a stack out of cards, which can break and scatter with just one blow.

So, choose permanence. Don't fall for the fake pursuit of happiness. Positive or negative doesn't matter. Deal with every emotion you feel truthfully. The real you matters. Stay true to yourself.

They left you, they cheated on you, they lied to you, they hurt you, even after loving so much, this tragedy happened. You trusted them and they broke your trust. This one person you trusted more than anyone else ever. That one person also proved you wrong.

Now the question here is, how can you trust people at all?

No, you can't trust people, you trust their actions. Actions guide you. Don't take a chance on people, take your chance based on their actions.

You only see yourself
incapable of trusting again
until someone tries to
win your trust again.
Honestly, you're just waiting
for another faithful person
to put your faith in.
There's no last chance
to trust, to believe,
however you fool yourself.
I would say,
faith can be shaken
but never destroyed.

—The idea of a last chance is an illusion

I understand, you loved them, more than enough, but that doesn't mean you don't love yourself, my girl.

Yes, they were the most important in that relationship but that doesn't mean you weren't. Yes, they said they deserved you and asked, can we try just one more time? And you gave in to them.

But now remember,
Second chances are not always about giving a chance to them. Sometimes, it can also go the other way round. Sometimes, by leaving them you might be giving a second chance to yourself.

Maybe we love better the second time? Maybe, the first love gushed into your life when you didn't even understand what love is or how to love. In fact, you didn't even know how to love yourself. Back then, you were figuring out almost everything. So, it's okay if it took you a while to realize that this person is not for you. This person is not your final destination. Maybe, you deserve another chance and a better love. Please don't feel guilty for the heartbreak you had to go through.

Maybe we love better the second time.

My heart and soul are filled with fire.
But my words and voice have found a way
to forgive you.
You may have hurt me
but I do not give you the permission
to break me.
And if you think
I'll be filled with hatred and pain,
you're wrong.
Because the next time I love,
I'll love harder and better.

We don't need a reason to be happy,
but we do need a reason
to escape what makes us unhappy.

Who knows?
Maybe
the heart breaks
for us to find
the treasure
full of self-love
hidden inside.

—Take a handful of that found treasure
and fix yourself

Whatever love you're giving, it's just going into someone's heart and nowhere else. So don't mind giving love. Don't regret whom you loved. Keep pouring. Whoever is receiving it won't be able to forget the way you loved. Sooner or later, it will come back to you. The value, the acknowledgement, the admiration, and the realization. All will be yours.

Keep loving.

Self-love is learnt
after a failed self
in love.

Always remember the reasons that keep you alive every day. Because no matter what, the hard truth is someone or the other in your life will give you a scar. Knowingly or unknowingly, they will disappoint you. Accept this fact and find your options to survive through this. Because you matter. You are needed. For some, you might be nothing, but for some, you are their everything. You are hope. Choose to live.

Praying to the Universe

Dear Universe,

I feel so stuck at the moment, being in this darkness is so painful, I don't like being like this. I didn't choose to be here. I have been dragged into this. But my faith in you hasn't been destroyed. I'd like to believe that maybe it's you who has blindfolded me for the surprises of joy ahead. I trust you.

With this enormous faith in you, now I can look beyond this pain and imagine how I'm jumping in the joy of your gifts presented to me. And now, even if it hurts, I'm okay. I will wait patiently to see what you have been planning for me while I was blindfolded.

How did I let one person out of a billion screw my life? I always counted less on myself for that one person. Yet, they left. It was awful to even see the way they left. I grieved, I cried, and I felt all the hurt and brokenness. But now I have to get back the power they took with them.

Dear Universe, I did no good to myself. I should've done better. But now I want to be healed. I'm worthy of this life, and I think this is your way of teaching me to value the self in me. And if it is so, I trust your way. I will take one step each day to love myself. I will give my self the worth it deserves.

I know you don't wake up and pray to God that you need suffering today. It comes out of the blue, by chance, uninvited. And whatever's unexpected we're not ready to face that. But even if you're not, don't pray to the Universe to skip this phase of your life. Instead, ask for the courage to deal with it and move on from this phase. Without facing the pain, you won't move ahead. What if there's something better further down? Pass through this road and see what happens next.

Why do we need hope and healing? I don't need it.
I don't want to see the day. I want to stay curled
up under this blanket till my tears dry up. I wish
the night lasted longer. After saying it all, suddenly
my inner voice knocked and told me that the world
doesn't end here. You shouldn't either. You have
waited for a long time without giving up on yourself.
Isn't it the hope of the future that has held you? Don't
hold on to the night. Let it pass, wake up, see the
day. See how things are moving and blooming. Don't
unsee it. You're missing out on the joy. You have seen
enough nights, now walk towards the sunlight and
you will see nothing remains the same. This hope in
your heart will heal you. Hope is the healing.

Listen, it's okay if you're not able to fight alone. You don't have to all the time. Just pray for the right person to knock at your door and guide you. Life is not all cruel and hopeless and impossible. The right people in your life will change the definition of life for you. Ask the Universe for an angel. It's okay to hold on to somebody. Just don't give up.

Break those walls
that you built around your heart.
Enough of this pretence,
lower your guard now,
let's remove the layers
of who you're not.
While you remove each brick
you'll realize,
how much you missed
being loved.
Put yourself out there
there are hearts
that would hold you in their embrace.
Ask for a better love
and you'll be bestowed with the best.

I promise.

Mark my words, in times of disbelief, unbelievable things will happen.

Don't surrender to the situation, don't let fate take control. Don't let anxiety smash your gut. Pray to the Universe. Try for what you truly want and the Universe will be forced to grant you what you deserve.

Believe, manifest, act and make it happen.
Mark my words. Just don't surrender. Make it happen.

It's easy to be patient and hope for the best
when things are okay and life is okay.
But what do you do when it gets dark
and you are lost and lonely?
How do you still carry the faith?
I think the answer is simple.
By knowing that no matter what happens,
you will end up exactly where you supposed to.
Maybe the only choice we are left with
is trusting the Universe and its flow.
So let go of everything and
simply trust the Universe.
Always.

When we look back, we don't say what happened was wrong or it shouldn't have happened. In fact, we are always grateful somewhere that the event took place for us to become who we are now. I think we all know that some events necessarily happen to bring out the best in us. Like when you were left alone, it was for you to discover that it's enough just for you to love yourself. You are enough to fight for yourself. We all know it. Don't we? You see, nothing in this Universe is irrelevant. Every single moment makes sense for something. Believe. Let it happen.

Death is the only end,
everything else in between is a process.

—*Trust the Universe and its flow*

Finding an Angel

Do not stop meeting humans,
do not stop being kind to them.
Angels too, take human form,
dropping their wings
walking on Earth
somewhere around you,
and you never know
when you might cross paths
with one of them.

I've met
quite a few humans till now
each one represented
a part of me.
Some reminded me
of the forgotten
and some
of the existing
some glimpses
caught me up in the hurt again
while some of them
healed and dropped me back again
in these complexities of going back and forth
can we ever be fixed completely?
Not really,
but we can be mended enough.
If some people break you
there are some
who'll help you mend yourself.
I believe,
people fix people.
At least the right ones do.

I don't need you to love you
but I do need you to love my self.

—Be my guardian angel

If you find someone
who never lets the kid inside you die
who has all the answers to your whys,
who has all the fire to add to your curiosity,
who becomes the words to your expressions,
who gives you everything that you asked
and never asked for,
who converts all your wrongs into rights,
who helps you live the way you're supposed to live.
If you find that someone, then give them everything.
Because
That someone is the angel you were searching for.

It took a quarter of my life
for someone to call me BEAUTIFUL
and I asked

'Why? How can you say that?
Tell me one thing that's beautiful in me.'

'I see a reflection of my soul in you
So to me, if I am beautiful, then
to me, you're beautiful too.'
And I was convinced.

—An angel's perspective

Some mornings you don't feel like waking up and when you open your eyes you are in tears thinking, why did the dawn even arrive?

You have to wake up and start with your routine. Meanwhile, the day is preparing to give you something entirely different. Suddenly you feel lighter, less heavy than yesterday.

Why?

'Cause even with tears, you had faith in your eyes for the new day. Even if the day appeared the same you decided to react in a new way.

It's not every day, it's a new day. Every day it's a new you with new emotions, new hope, new shine, new faith and new reasons to keep yourself alive.

Take a chance on this day. Things might change

—Hope sent in an envelope by an angel

You are my stepping stone. The world pulled me and dragged me down, where they thought I belonged, but you didn't give up on me. Your hand was firm enough to pull me up and help me stand where I actually belonged. Thank you for existing. I am what I am because of who you are. Thank you for re-birthing me.

—*Grateful*

Surrender.

The word sounds so submissive, but let me tell you,
there's nothing more powerful that your soul can do
if it knows how to surrender.

Now, why do we devote ourselves to someone?
Why do we surrender to someone?
And what is the greatest surrender?

I think it's love. For love.

Only through surrender can you understand love,
and understand yourself. Surrender means putting
away the doubts, fears, hatred, temptations that
can bruise you or someone else. Put down that ego,
expectations, and past experiences. Give all of you.
Do not hold back.

You know, although surrender is an act of giving,
the returns on it is abundance. An abundance of
happiness, joy and peace. Trust me on this and
surrender.

Yes, you sank her into your darkness.
Yes, you trapped her.
But
Now she is a goddess
who found an angel.
Her voice lit up his heart.
She illuminated, eventually
turning the angel into a moon
gave him a purpose.
From darkness they rose
she became a Phoenix,
and he a Pegasus.
What a celestial transformation.

Believe it or not, but I think
there's an angel for every goddess.
An angel who will hold a mirror for you
and make you see
the prettiest and the most magical side of you.
Do not give up.
Wait for your angel.
Till then, be your own angel.
Will you?

Gone are the days
when the centre of our Universe
would be me.
I loved making your heart throb
with my mere presence
but eventually you broke
the idea of permanence.
Maybe to remind me
That what I'm seeking will not be mine forever
Only my soul will last with me.
So, this time,
let me find a goddess
to hold my hand
and be my strength.
Standing by me
And living within me.

GODDESS

Goddess Awakens

I searched in people,
so many people,
I exhausted my entire self in this search
but nobody could bring me back,
from the circle
of pain, sorrow, grief, anxiety, tears and bad luck.
that's when I was forced to ignite what's inside me
what nobody could do, I did it for myself
I found a way to peace
I found the lost key
and unlocked the force
it wasn't there in people to find
it was buried in me
now it's time, I glow
whether you burn or shine with my light
is none of my concern
I won't let this light fade even a bit
I'm all alone this time
but I'm fiercer than ever.

—*Goddess has arrived*

A goddess is only a woke soul,
born to save the body of the lost girl.

Someone asked me, who is a goddess?

I think a goddess is no one but a girl who completely knows, accepts and believes in herself. A lost girl who found the mystics of her soul.

They asked me again,

Why do you think every girl is a goddess?

'Cause every girl is me, and if I can see the goddess in me, why can't every girl around me look for a goddess in them? Don't you think so?

I remember the day the girl in me burst into tears and cried and cried till she felt choked. She was unable to look at herself, no more confidence to talk to anyone outside the room. All lost. All alone. Forgotten.

But when she sipped the first cup of coffee, she heard something,

'Knock knock . . . Listen girl, you're a goddess, goddess is you. Own YOU. The world might not give a damn about the girl in you, but they will have to worship the goddess in you. Remember the times you sprinkled your goddess-ness and they were spellbound by your untamed energy? Do you remember? How did that happen? Wasn't that you?'

The goddess in her awakened.

Every time I was about to reach the finish line, they compelled me to lag behind, they compelled me to take a U-turn. But it's high time now; I can't let them mould my destiny any more. I will try my hardest to become who I wanted to become. You cut my wings and I will stitch them on again. It's time to armour those wings. Time to switch from a girl to a goddess.

The girl cries in her
dark room
looking at the light.
The window of the future
brings her a message.
Sketch your own wings and kiss skies,
take off from the ground,
leave those people just there
with their critical opinions and ruthless voices.
You create your heaven
where you are free from
someone dressing down you
someone crying down you
someone tearing down you.
And I know
the day that home is built
you will carve a name
on a wooden plate
which would read
'a goddess's abode'.

I'm not just my bones and skin. I'm not just what your eyes can see. And I'm not alone even if it seems so. I might look weak and fragile, but I carry a force within me. It is the energy inside me that fixed me every time I got broken. It's the divine force that kept me going. And I'm grateful to that divine force which has always guided me. Now all I know is, it deserves to be worshipped.

So, I call that divine force, 'the goddess in me'.

Do you know why the goddess is needed?

When so many people want to get a hold of you.
When some tie your thoughts, some your voice, and
some your time.
A roar, a scream, a voice with loud words is needed
against them.
To be free from the life they want to give you.
And I don't know anyone else apart from the goddess
residing in me that can do this.

Awaken the goddess inside you.
You are your only help.

It's funny how we blame the world for everything that happens to us. For our hurt, our pain, our misery, our sorrow, and everything that's not in our favour. We blame the world. But you know what, the world doesn't really know us enough to be able to cause us trouble. We are affected by very few people who reside in this world. Our emotions are overpowered by only those few. Think of yourself as more than those people. Instead of listening to their noise, listen to the music of your soul. There's a goddess that resides in you. It's guiding you every single day.

—*The realization*

Goddess Realizes

I wandered through life.
Unimportant, unseen, unknown.
I kept asking myself,
'Why can't people see me?
What does it take to be seen, heard and understood?'

And I realized,
I needed to stop looking outside.
And start looking inside me.
If I could see, hear, and understand myself,
everyone else would.

How simple it was.

She was loved loathingly. They loved as if they were
doing her a favour. They made her feel she was
unlovable, unworthy and should thank her stars that
they even chose to love her. The girl lost herself in
their filthy idea of love and kept giving her body,
mind and heart to the undeserving ones. She chose to
stay there. Powerless.

But after a while, the goddess in her awakened. She
realized, 'to love her is to worship her'.

She loves fiercely, enormously, and devotedly
only when the person mirrors the depth of her love.
Give her all the love back in an avalanche.
Make her say, 'Wow! Is this how much I deserved to
be loved?'

Love is not blind. In fact, love makes us see things we could never see. Love knows what's right and what's wrong. Love is not an influence. Love is an identity of our soul. How can it go wrong? Love awakens you. Misguided are those who deceive love. The ones who have seen through love, guide people that love is the only right. Love is not blind. So, don't blame love, blame people who never understood the divinity of love.

Stop feeling. Stop expressing. I told my heart as
a broken girl. But then I realized, if I keep myself
deprived from feeling anything just because I'm scared
of getting hurt, I won't ever be able to feel the real
love in my life. If the right love knocks at my heart
and if I don't let it enter and absorb it into my bones,
I will always be deprived of love. And I will always be
left broken.

—*Accept, express and embrace*

I was never called a princess, like other daughters.
I wasn't raised by a man.
I was never loved.
Why was I chosen for this kind of life?
This question bothered me so much.
But then I heard a scream inside me.

'You were not called a princess because
you are a goddess.'

This voice had always been your protector.
Celebrate your strength. You were nurtured by your
own soul. You aren't someone's princess but you're
everyone's goddess.

Maybe you are not searching for someone special.
Maybe who you are really seeking is someone that
makes you realize that you are special.
Very often, we love others so we can try to love
ourselves. So stupid of us that we need others to value
ourselves.

Always build two homes for yourself.

One inside your heart and one inside them.
Take care of both homes equally.
Nurture both with love.
Spend time in both homes.
So, in case one day you are left homeless by them,
you still have a home left inside your heart.
You know your home will always welcome you
wherever you go. You won't lose your way.

You are secured by your own self. Isn't it beautiful?

—*The warning*

Why do we need wounds to realize the value of that person or that relationship? Why do we hold on until we get hurt by the accident? We speed up things for the momentary adrenaline. We speed up our relationship and forget to pause at the red sign. You know that you can escape by stopping at the red sign. Yet you don't, you disregard everything else visible around you in this thrill ride.

Love for real teaches patience in the adventure. It won't hurt too much if you could patiently observe the journey. If you could see where you are heading to.

—*Pause at the red sign*

Changing them isn't your task. Just because you love them. Yes, in love we accept the person as they are. But if something hurts you, it should be changed. They can't be let off with the excuse that this is them and they have been like this since forever.

Yes, it doesn't matter how the person was before meeting you. But it does matter now. 'Cause now your strings are attached to them. Every action of theirs impacts you. They are responsible for the acts that impact you.

We can't hold ourselves responsible for loving them. Never fall in guilt. You're not supposed to be a forgiver all the time, just for the sake of their corrupted love.

Why do people fail in love?

I think, the day, you take love for granted,
you are bound to fail.

Why is it sometimes more difficult to stay and easier to leave?

I think it's because we always see the impossibility of staying and the possibility of leaving. But never the possibility of staying and the impossibility of leaving.

If there's an easy way out, there's also an easy way in. Take my word, love is the easiest thing to do if only you know how to do it.

Do you think we ever fall out of love?

That's not possible. We are made from love.
In some or the other way, we are always immersed in
love. Some are in love with the divine and others with
the humans made by the divine. There's no way a
person can fall out of love.

So, don't get fooled if someone says, I have fallen
out of love. They might have fallen out of love with
a person but at the same moment they are falling in
love with another. No human can stay deprived of
love.

We are love and we will run on love till our last
breath.

No matter how it ended, even in your hatred, there are some bits of them that you have loved, and you will continue to love. It could be a gesture, an expression, or anything that they have done for you. Something that you'll always miss and that you might not find in anyone else.

Try to carry that part of theirs in you and reflect it to the world in a nice way. That's how you keep them with you. That's how you love and forgive. That's how beautiful your soul is.

Each time I think about this, it leaves me teary-eyed.
Why do people limit their definition of beauty to the
structure of our skeleton, the shimmer on the skin
and the shape of the body?

Why couldn't they see what my eyes dreamt, what my
words meant, what my voice felt, what my heart held
and what my soul searched for?

But then I realize, they didn't judge me, I let them.
And so now it stops. I decide my own terms of
beauty.

And I see, *we all are goddamn beautiful.*

As a girl, one morning, I climbed up a mountain to see a god's idol. Seeking for truth, seeking answers. I went with a chaotic mind filled with questions, demands and complaints.

But the moment I saw His eyes, I cried with tears. Nothing to say, ask or want. Just a contented heart.

Later, I pondered, and everything made sense. The joy is in the divine's presence. He wants nothing, you want nothing. Both are there for nothing. That's the joy. All the desires I had weren't mine. I picked them from some person or the other that I'd met in life. If my desires were truly mine, I would have asked for them to be fulfilled but my soul didn't want anything.

I am a happy being with nothing.

That's the truth. Realizing this truth will bring you joy.

Self-love is not an expression
but it is an acceptance.

You cannot borrow love from somebody, and you cannot ask others as a favour to shower love on you. It starts with you. For how long will you keep hating yourself? Yes, it is okay to work on things you don't like about yourself, but that doesn't mean you worsen it by hating yourself. You'll have to stop this or else it'll take away your life.

Self-love is not expensive, it is basic.
You just have to accept the person you already are.

Someone asked me, what would you do if you became a real divine goddess with supernatural powers?

I think, if that ever happens, I would like to make a chip that has all the solutions to all the possible and impossible problems. After making that chip, I would really like to fix it in human souls. So that they are compelled to look inside them to find out the answers and get rid of the trouble.

I know for a fact that not every solution is out there in the world. But you can find a solution to every and any problem when you look inside yourself.

Try to find the angel/goddess inside you.
The light is in you, don't waste your time seeking it outside.

Goddess Fights

I kept on asking myself why I fear some people. Why am I always scared to face them? I tried to think about it and it came to me.

Maybe because I think they are powerful. But ironically, they're not powerful. I have given them the power to scare me. I decided I should take back that power and give it to the person it belongs to, and I realized that's me. I will take that power back and give it to myself.

My head is always filled with self-doubts. I'm so indecisive. It's suffocating to wonder, why can't I rely on myself? Why can't I decide what's best for me? Is it that difficult? Or is it the labels I got from people over the years that have shattered my confidence completely? I think it's time I remove these tags, one by one. I need to be myself once again. I'll have to learn to live on my own terms.

Why doesn't anyone seem to pause? Why am I being pushed to achieve greater after greater after greater things?

Sometimes I feel I don't want the greater gifts from the Universe if it doesn't let me hold on to the ones I already have. I don't want to move faster. I want to take my time. I want to feel a bit more. I want those old things again. I want time to freeze. I know I'm going nowhere with such questions, but these thoughts, they don't seem to stop, and the only way I know is to sit and have my moment with them. I will have to pause.

He thought
she was a muse
and may become
a heroine someday.
But she wanted to
prove him wrong.
She carried
the will in her veins
to be a superheroine
saving not just the world
but her own self
one day.

Suddenly everything's a question.

Do you really own yourself? Have you ever got a chance to own yourself?

Since you were born, even your own name has been GIVEN to you. From that day on, you have been living a life owned by someone else, your parents or your guardian. Yes, those days as a girl, it didn't cost too much to be owned by someone else. But now you're a woman, do you want to be owned forever or make your own identity?

So, today, take your life in your hands. Yes, they had a habit of owning you since you were born, but now, for once, try owning yourself.

Fight for the woman in you. Power the goddess in you.

With the goddess inside me,
I know I'm worth my every breath.

—*Inhale life*

Don't choose silence
It won't speak on your behalf.

—Volume up

It's dark
but it won't be forever.
The light comes through
when we need it the most.
Just keep the window open.
Just keep the heart open.

—This too shall pass

Only when you don't know how to love yourself, do you want someone to do that for you. So, if they do that, you're good, but if they don't, you breakdown into pieces. You crumble. Remember, love's destruction is self-destruction.

So, instead of asking someone to love you, protect yourself by discovering the love you have for yourself. Love for the self is the only saviour.

The Universe paired the energies. Sun and moon, dark and light, earth and sky. They're perfect. And then we humans paired our emotions. We paired love with hate. But isn't that wrong? Instead, we must pair love and life. Because life happens only when we breathe love. And then we paired hatred with heartbreak. We must pair hatred and hurt. Because hatred lives in hurt's home. Don't mess it up.

—*Open your eyes*

Between life and death
every doing is a choice
use your free will.

—*Nothing is predestined*

Goddess Endures

Why should we endure the pain?
It's because, even endure says

end-your-pain.

I still remember the feeling of my first heartbreak.
I remember how soul-shattering the experience was.
How I felt that the nerves in my head would tear up
and my body would never be able to move. I almost
considered it the end of my life. It's funny that it has
now become a once-upon-a-time story. Today, the
feelings have been neutralized. I neither pray for nor
curse that person. In fact, I don't think about that
person every time I dress up any more. This makes me
realize that the Universe has given us all the ability
to repair and you can use that ability by choosing
forgiveness.

—*Goddess endures*

We're all carrying a lot of trauma within us right now. We're all desperate to share it with someone and in need of easing that pain a bit. But let me tell you this, one day we all will reach a place where we would be kind of 'okay' with any such pain, because we would know nothing is permanent. Everything fades in the end. Wait for that day, you won't need anyone to share your pain with.

—The truth about life

To all,
Devastated, heartbroken, choking-in-pain people.
I want you to remember
we are all born in pain
we have all been raised with pain.
But I also want you to remember
just like pain,
we are also gifted with endurance.
Endure.
In the end, you will triumph.
Endure.
Not for others
But to triumph in the love
That you lost for yourself.

I feel your grief. Today you are questioning your existence, but I ask you to just once think and answer yourself, 'whatever I had to face or struggle with, would I have wanted it any other way?'

When you look back on the past, everything makes sense, and so today, too, hold on, even if it doesn't seem easy. Because tomorrow I'm sure you will be grateful for everything that's happening with you now.

Don't pity yourself, keep your head high and just walk through this situation.

You know, whenever I have some time alone, I laugh like a mad person looking at the times we spent together. And while laughing, I suddenly shed tears which become uncontrollable, because I know I can't bring you back.

But that's okay. I can bear these tears but not you any more. I can live with your memories but I cannot stand your presence. All I know now is that it's okay to feel the after-effects of a person who was once your habit. The body will take time to adapt to the new version of myself. I can't force things to change overnight for me. And yes, I do understand that no pain can last after a period of time. One day, I will have my piece of peace.

Lingering in an enormous, isolated pad,
counting its square foot every day,
With my routine folks and a neighbourhood where,
who lives doesn't concern any more.
I reminisce about the days when I used to live in the
street
where the spaces didn't matter as much as the people
did.
Two hundred houses in one lane
Each house connected to one another, as much as the
hearts of the residents,
Jumping from one patio to the tenth was every day's
entertainment.

Back in the time,
when every summer the bell of an ice popsicle caravan
was heard
And every winter the smell of enticing corn felt.
Every night, when the clock struck eight,
Out came the notorious kids of the street
Annoying the peeps with their irritating screams and
laughter,
Some suffered as sin, while many found it sweet

But,
As the time flew,
My physical self began to fight
transforming hormones,

witnessing heinous monsters coming my way,
The gentleman who someday took me in his lap
Has become lecherous
Prying on the growing bust
Of girls turned women.
My heart cribs,
When romancing a man
Who regarded them as whore.

Gone are the days, when this street was the whole
world.
I don't belong to that place any more.
The street unfit me,
While
The apartment perplexes me,
Where do I belong?
What do I deserve?
I dived deep in the thoughts
To find a shelter to pre-empt,
pre-empt from the toxic world. And
it came back in silence and whispered in my ears,
'Rush to your soul,
To reach your self's abode.'

I'm glad you didn't choose to stay.
If you had stayed, what we would have built wasn't
going to be worth living anyway. I'm in a much better
space now. It must be hard for you to believe that I
did choose to stay alive without you. But trust me,
I'm doing good. I'm rebuilding the home inside my
heart that you once destroyed. This time I'm making
sure my door is concrete and allows only permanence.

Don't find reasons to numb your pain. Once and for all feel it. See what's broken inside and feel it the way it is. Don't wound what is already wounded by numbing it. It's your body, your heart, your soul. Feel it and fix it.

Do you know the back story of your birth?
I'll tell you mine.

I was resting in my safest place, my mother's womb.
Mumma had to visit Ahmedabad in her seventh
month of pregnancy. She was at the railway station.
She went to the loo and everything around her started
getting unsteady. She thought she was dizzy after the
journey. But it was the buzz of people pushing each
other and rushing to get out of the station which
made her realize that the unsteadiness was the result
of an earthquake. She, with her heavy body and
a suitcase, started running to save me and herself.
Her heart was pounding but she didn't stop and
eventually got out of that place. I was saved and kept
safe in her womb.

How important was I to this world, I realized after
hearing this story. I was meant to be. We all, whoever
is here in this world, are meant to be. We belong to
this world. The Universe wanted us.

Ask your mom about the worth of your existence. We
really have no right to scratch or bruise or snatch the
soul out of this body. Don't convince yourself that
you don't matter to this world. Believe your birth-
giver. Believe your very own goddess.

Transcend the body
See through me,
I'm BEAUTIFUL
I'm a GODDESS
I'm an ANGEL.

—Say it out loud

Goddess Hearts

A lot of people around you in your life are here with
you for a limited time. Very few of them choose
to extend that limited time and stay with you for
longer. And only those who stay beyond that time are
rightfully yours.
yours to keep,
yours to get attached to,
and yours to love.

No love should be worth the hurt. We should stop fooling ourselves and keep accepting hurt and keep taking pain and justify it all by thinking it is for the sake of love. True love doesn't involve hurt. It doesn't involve torture, fights, tears, and all the drama and trauma. In fact, true love should sort everything out for you. It should make you a nice human. It should fill your life with smiles, and a lot of it. So, I would say, don't accept being hurt for love. Take only love for love.

If you really want to love better the next time and want to be loved the best all over again, then forgive wholeheartedly. It's not easy, but it's necessary for you to look forward to loving again. I hope you do that for your own sake.

It's not about choosing the right love.
It's about choosing the right person
to love and be loved.
By the right person
I mean the one
who understands you,
respects you,
and accepts you
for what you are.
when you find that right person,
I think love will never leave you.

Now when I'm in love I question myself,
Do I remember who or how I was before?
No.
Do l like this version of myself more now?
Yes.
But why?
Because loving you helped me find a purpose of us
being with each other. We are here to complete each
other's jigsaw, the final piece that's needed to feel
complete. But that is not it.
Our journey doesn't end here. After completing the
jigsaw, we have to protect it from the world's evil eye.
No other voice should confuse it again and take it
away from us. So yes, we will have to lead with love
not just today but for all the coming tomorrows.

Whether you believe it or not
we're a chosen pair.
We can only be seen together
we become invisible as individuals.
Our union is an ode
That the Universe echoes.
It's an answer to the souls
who question the need for a soulmate.

Deep down I knew that you were the one for me.
How? The day we met for the first time and after a
few minutes of talking, looking into my eyes you said,

'I'm liking who you are now, but to be honest, this
is not you. You have guarded yourself with a lot of
layers. I think if I can like the pretence of you then I
think I will also be in love with the real you.'

That's it. You said it and I fell for it.
That's when I knew, you were the one for me.

—*You saw me quite literally*

I think perfect love exists. It doesn't matter how imperfect or perfect you are. If two people become clay and if they let the Universe mould them and love shape them, then what they'll have between them won't be seen as anything less than perfect.

Trust me, love can shape all the imperfections and make two people look flawless and heavenly.

You loved me
and I forgot if I've ever been loved before.
You touched me
and I forgot if I've ever been touched before.
You kissed me
and I forgot if I've lived in this same world before.
I've known people,
you aren't like them.
Tell me what kind are you?

Love is more of invention and less of fear.
We invent names for each other.
We invent ways to treat each other.
And fears? What even is that?
A non-dancer dances like no one's watching,
an inexpressive person writes a whole poem for the
other,
an aromantic person goes on his knees in front of
hundreds.
Fall in love once.
Not just because you'll overcome fears,
it'll make you do unthinkable, unimaginable things.
Drench wholly and bask in the glory of love.

'You know me so well,' you said.

It's because I observe 'what' you inhale.
And I observe 'how' you exhale.
I hear your breath.
It tells me things you don't say.

Promises fossilized:

I promise to embarrass you with all the possible
cheesy gestures.
I promise to squeeze you, cling to you, even when not
needed.
I promise to say you I Love You from the time I wake
up to the time I hit the sack.
I promise to claim you always as 'mine'.
I promise to kiss you at all the places we ever travel
to.
I promise to wine only with you.
I promise to make love with the sunrise and the
moonsets.
I promise to deservedly possess you.
I promise to say to you always 'How stunning you
look, the world envies you.'
I promise to bleed the love you deserve.
I promise to tour our love across the globe.
I promise to write you.
Lastly,
I promise to breathe you.

'The promises we made wrapped in the blanket,
holding hands, under the stars.'

—*Celebration of love*

You know why one person is enough to love and be loved for life?

'Cause after hustling an entire life for love, your tired soul wants to shelter in a home that will grow old with you. Something that's irreplaceable, and when you find your home in a person and when they allow you to own them, you make your permanent residence there. And when you have your permanent address, why would you go for rentals? Why won't you rather decorate your own house with little things that make it look more beautiful every passing day?

—*My permanent address—you*

You equalled your 'I love you' with a smile in your eyes and a kiss on my forehead.
You equalled your 'I love you' by rolling tears with gratitude for my existence.
You equalled your 'I love you' by prioritizing me in us.
You equalled your 'I love you' by inhaling me before inhaling air.

This is the you I dreamed of.
You're my miraculous manifestation.

We all think of a life where we're not bound with anyone or by anyone. We all want to be free to decide whom to love and whom not to love. We just don't want to be stuck. But somehow, we're unable to, right?

I want to ask you, isn't it beautiful to be someone's home? By asking for such a life, we're just moving out of the home and reaching nowhere. The truth is, we all enjoy the journey thinking that it has a beautiful destination.

Find a home and be a home to someone. Bound in love with someone. Forever is beautiful.

The other night, he said, 'Some days our intimacy feels so deep that I don't feel like leaving your body.'

I asked, 'Why? What makes you feel like that?'

He replied,

'If there is one way I could feel, that I'm you and you're me, that we both are made from the same stardust, that I and you have been and will be together, forever, it is this way. Our bodies, minds, hearts and souls consumed by each other. We feel one and we hate to break that. We hate to get divided into two individuals again.

'Intimacy makes us stars emitting light. Intimacy makes us gods and goddesses.'

When two things merge with each other
everlasting awe takes place.
Like when darkness merges with light and
when the light merges with darkness
the dusk and dawn arrive.
When the earth and the sky meet
we see a horizon
and the union is breathtaking.
I wonder,
if you and I don't just collide
but also
meet and merge
what would the Universe create?

—*A new Universe*

Goddess Wins

You balanced me. You held me so I don't sway away in my temptations, my vices, my voices, and my itch. I wonder how you did that. How did you not let me lose myself once again? I think now I know who you are.

You are *Love*. Thank you for bringing *You* in my life.

I found myself.

—Thank you, goddess

NISHI

Time changes everything, you know why?

'Cause even when you're stuck and numb after getting
broken, you're still constantly moving, meeting
people and you're observing those people resembling
what you have gone through, those people are helping
you rebuild your lost hope. And that's how flowing
with time, a person, a day, or a moment helps you
find your answers, and once again you're ready to try
and work things out for yourself in a better way.

So, take it easy. Let time flip things for you.

—*Wait and win*

Someone told me to be myself in all ways. I'm a gorgeous creation. I'm one of those rare findings that people long for, that people look for their entire life. So, if I lose myself, then how will they find a creation like me? 'Cause there isn't any goddess like me. Don't lose yourself. You are only one. There isn't anybody else like you.

—*Owning it, winning it*

Ever heard the saying, 'Dance like no one's watching'? But you know, when you do dance like no one's watching, someone watches you. And that someone falls for you so hard, that he ends up being music to your steps for life.

All I'm saying is, reflect what's in your heart, some hearts will find it adorable. Be you. It's attractive.

'Add compromise in your life, someday you'll have to compromise, somewhere you'll have to compromise and with someone you'll have to compromise.'

In my head, I felt like punching the faces who told me to do so. But this girl, so weak, could only listen to this word, 'compromise', and cry.

After all, it takes a goddess in you to kick this word out and tell the world, 'If I'm born as a goddess, I deserve none but an angel. I deserve a place nothing less than a heaven, no person with an idea of compromise deserves to surround me. I dare you to make me settle for less.'

I'm a freaking goddess.

You don't have to fight with the world
to become a goddess,
you just have to make your scars worth it.

You don't have to boast about yourself to the world
to become a goddess,
you have to simply love yourself
enough to fix the girl in you.

You don't have to be an attention-receiver
to become a goddess,
you just have to esteem the divinity in you
for people to honour it.

It doesn't take much to become a goddess,
does it?

Goddess Writes

I have stopped running away from it.
Instead,
I have started preparing for my death.
For when my body is not around
you can still count on me
I want to remind you
that you are connected to my soul
and this connection surpasses births and deaths.
I want to remind you
that even after my body turns into ashes
I will be there for you
always
In some or the other form
because
I'm not this physique
I'm not just a girl
I'm beyond
I'm my soul
I'm the force.
I'm a goddess.

Nobody is incapable of loving. They're just not choosing you as their priority. Each one of us is in love with something or someone. But it is always about the priority. You choose the one whose sole priority is to love you with all their capacity. In this world with a billion people, you deserve at least one soul that knows how to love you more than anyone else, and trust me, that is possible. You just have to make a choice whenever you have a chance.

After everything you've gone through,
If you still think about the person from your past
I would say there's nothing wrong with it.
Because why not,
sometime in the past
that person meant so much to you.
You shared a connection with that person.
So, you are allowed to walk down that memory lane.
Shed a tear, cry out loud or smile about the fact that
you've grown from those difficult times. Zone out
from this moment and feel free to take yourself into
those days in the past.
It's okay to do so for a while
but then
also bring yourself back to the present
and remember
that if you are on the journey of going forward, you
can't invest too much of your time in looking back.
I hope you understand.

I know you have been unloved for a long time. Nothing makes sense to you, not yesterday and not even today. But I want to tell you, you don't have to look back, you just have to look forward.

Create hope in your heart and it's okay even if it's not true. Fool your heart today and convince it that soon it is going to receive lots of love from places you never imagined. Who knows, all of it might come true.

Life always has more to offer, and nobody can deny that. Okay?

Three things I realized on my journey towards self.

1. You can't wait for the light to find you; you must move towards the light with your aching heart to heal yourself.
2. Process your pain to be able to set yourself free from it. Endure it.
3. Remember your body is the Universe's gift and you have no right to degrade it.

Love doesn't have any destination
yet it takes you everywhere
from cloud nine to rock bottom
through pain and breakdowns
to ecstasy, to anxiety
but no matter what,
in the end, love still prevails
and offers you peace and delight
that is why,
don't shy away from experiencing love
don't be afraid of it
for you'll never be short of love
nobody can steal it away from you.
love is an everlasting essence,
That you'll find in yourself
sooner or later.

Me to myself:

There's no way one can read you. Sometimes you're nonchalant and other times you're chaotic. Sometimes you become the creator of an art, sometimes you become an art. You're a Universe in yourself whose existence I can't question but can only look at in wonder and awe. Observing your thousand shades, this time I'm trying to write about the Universe, and I'm revolving the closest.

Hey, why would you say,
What you write is not enough?
What you speak is not enough?
What you share is not enough?
What you own is not enough?
Try to understand, whatever it is,
it's your experience of life through your eyes.
Don't underrate it.
The feeling of
'I am enough'
is the secret to never being stuck.

You know what,
words will make a lot of things believable.
but your gut,
your instincts,
that feeling won't lie.
If you sense it is wrong
then no words should shadow
or overpower that sense.
Don't let the voice within you sleep,
when it has come to wake you up.

Love is an art gifted to each one of us. An art that is born to be expressed and not kept inside, away from the eyes of the world.

Love truly is an art. It's you who haven't yet realized that you're an artist, deserving of holding this art. Admit it now that you're an artist, and keep creating this art with your heart and pass it on to the worthy ones. You owe it to yourself and them.

Someone asked me, what is the purpose of life?

Looking at the bustling city-view from my window, I thought about it and it came to me.

That all of us are chasing something or someone every day. We're trying to find, explore, discover everything in this world except ourselves. We were born and left puzzled between people, things, thoughts and emotions and forgot the purpose, which is, 'to find the self that's within, to know what's within'.

I realized that we're abundant in ourselves, that we're all enough. And that realization is probably the purpose of life.

It began with you
It was about you
It is within you
It will end with you.

—*Life*

When the sun sets on my side of the world
and leaves its colours behind
it makes me feel a little sad
but fills me with hope and peace
It paints the sky pink and orange
and all kinds of hues
even though it lasts for a few minutes
you know it will never leave you.
and even though it's dark here now
I know,
the sun is up on your side of the world.
it's never gone
forever.

and so I hope
just like the sun
when I bid my adieus to this world
I want to leave my words for people
to cherish and hold in their hearts
like I was never gone
like I'm still there in the form of a guiding light.
like I'm still there somewhere
waiting to re-arrive.

—*From the girl and the goddess*

Do you know why you're losing?
You might not be aware
But the light in you is dimming
You've tortured, drained,
weakened and shaken your entire self
You won't be able to fight longer
unless you empower the light within
This is your time,
The self inside you is craving your love
Pay attention,
You will see,
The wisdom you were seeking around the world
was with you all this time.
You were never alone
Your 'self' was backing you all the time
You have always been the creator
of your joy, sorrow, calm and melancholy
this is your time,
you create the unbreakable
remove the layers of who you are not
and allow yourself to take off
become alive again
let the glow of your light inside
spread across the world
bring your enormous self on the table
let them know
the goddess has arrived.

Epilogue

Dear goddess tribe,

I hope now you know that you're all more than what you think of yourself. You all are goddesses and angels beneath your exterior self. All this while, with the help of the goddess/angel, you have come this far. Although this energy, the force within you was unknown to you until now, it was always there. I believe you won't be lost any more if you keep fitting yourself in the shoes of a goddess/angel. A lot of you might have gone through what I, in my journey, have gone through. People came into your life, they went, they broke your heart, they left you without warning. But whatever happened, each time it triggered an alarm in you to protect yourself and continue your journey. That's the energy of your soul. The light in you can repair anything. You don't have to seek help from the Universe that's outside because what you have inside is even more vast. Don't see yourself as just one. You yourself are one whole Universe. Your higher self is your goddess/angel. I hope this book has been a discovery for your self. There isn't an angel outside to hold your hand. From now on, you hold your own hand. Hold firm. And you'll feel as though you have a friend walking alongside you and helping you walk through the roads that life has paved for you. Rely more on yourself. Trust your instincts. Believe in your calling.

I bow down in gratitude to all of you who stuck around through this entire journey of a girl unleashing the goddess in her. I hope together we can enlighten more souls and calm their restless minds. Share your learnings from this book with the ones who need guidance in their lives at this moment. Reach out to your fellow humans. Be their guiding force. Love and hugs.

—@goddesswrites

Acknowledgements

Thank you to my mom, Veeni, Shubham and everyone in the family for always loving me unconditionally and being so supportive. So much love for you.

Thank you, Ashish, my best friend, a true angel and the best poet I know. You helped me discover the goddess in me. This book would not have existed without you.

Thank you, Savi, for your feedback on this book and for always wishing the best for me.

My friends and followers, for appreciating my writings and loving me for what I am. Thank you for always being there.

Thank you everyone at Penguin Random House, my publisher, for believing in me and working so hard on publishing this book.

Forever grateful to the Universe.